THE BROTHERS

Reza de Wet
THE BROTHERS

OBERON BOOKS
LONDON

First published in 2006 by Oberon Books Ltd
521 Caledonian Road, London N7 9RH
Tel: 020 7607 3637 / Fax: 020 7607 3629
e-mail: info@oberonbooks.com
www.oberonbooks.com

A catalogue record for this book is available from the British Library.

ISBN: 1 84002 235 3

Cover design: Andrzej Klimowski

Printed in Great Britain by Antony Rowe Ltd, Chippenham.

To Lindsay
with profound gratitude for his invaluable insight
and advice during the writing of this text

Also to the memory of his remarkable brothers
Warwick and Fraser

'When my blanket falls off me at night, I begin to dream of enormous slippery rocks, the cold autumn water, the bare shores – all this is vague, in a mist, with not a fragment of blue sky… When I run away from the river, I pass the tumbledown cemetery gates, the funerals of my schoolmasters…'

Anton Chekhov describing his dreams about Taganrog

Characters

ANTON
twenty-nine, an attractive and graceful man with thick, brown hair and a soft beard. On the one hand, there is something evasive and elusive about him; on the other, he has a childlike spontaneity and is amused by the grotesque and the absurd. When he wishes to exercise it, he has an easy and natural charm.

ALEKSANDER
thirty-four, tall and angular. He is intense and extremely changeable. He often behaves irresponsibly and childishly.

NATALIA
thirty-three, with large, mournful eyes. She is pale and haggard, with vestiges of her former exotic fragility.

*This portrayal of the Chekhov family
is closely based on historical fact*

The Brothers was first performed at the Actors Centre, the Civic Theatre, Johannesburg in October 2004 with the following cast:

ANTON, Duncan Lawson

ALEKSANDER, André Stolz

NATALIA, Sylvaine Strike

WAILERS, Hermien de Vos & Corine Broomberg

Director Lynne Maree

Time 1889

Place A squalid country cottage (*dacha*) in the Ukraine where the Chekhov family are spending the summer.

The action takes place in the seedy and cramped living-room of the country house. At present the room is being used as Anton's bedroom and study. Centre left, a table with two chairs. A jacket hangs over the back of one of the chairs. A silk dressing-gown hangs on the back of the study door. There are papers strewn on the table, as well as an ink-well, a wooden blotter, a carafe and a glass. There is also a violin on the table. Against the back wall a narrow bed which has been made up for the night. Centre right, an old sofa and a large wicker chair. Against the right wall, a bureau with shelves. A window in the left wall is covered by a dingy lace curtain. There is a doctor's bag on the worn carpet near the sofa.

In the back wall are two doors. Both doors are reached by steps and a small landing. The door on the left leads to the bedroom where the body of Kolia lies in its coffin. When the door is opened, flickering candles can be glimpsed. The door on the right leads to the hall and the rest of the house. Downstage right, there is a door which leads to the dining-room.

Almost until the end of the play an oil-lamp burns above the table and candles burn in a candelabrum on the bureau.

Sound effects are of extreme importance. They have to sound completely realistic and be carefully orchestrated.

ACT ONE

It is 11 o'clock at night. A priest can be heard chanting softly behind the closed bedroom door. ANTON writing almost ferociously at the table. He is dressed in a shirt and an elegant, well-fitting pair of pants which he wears with braces. He wears a pince-nez while he writes.

ANTON: (*Muttering as he reads what he's written.*) 'He begins to descend more slowly.' No. (*Makes a correction.*) 'More and more slowly…'

Clattering of crockery in the dining-room.

NATALIA: (*Voice from the dining-room.*) You can't sleep with your head on the table. Wake up!

The sound of ALEKSANDER groaning loudly. ANTON lifts his head and listens.

And see what you've done. You've upset the gravy!

Sound of ALEKSANDER blowing his nose loudly.

Not on the napkin! What a pig you are!

ANTON chuckles.

(*Off.*) And on top of it all, there's borscht in your hair!

ALEKSANDER: (*Off. Growling.*) Leave me alone!

NATALIA: (*Hissing.*) Suit yourself!

ANTON: (*Chuckles again. Opens a small notebook and writes in it. Muttering as he writes.*) 'And on top of it all, there's borscht in your hair.' (*Closes the notebook and continues to write as before.*)

Silence. While ANTON writes the priest is still chanting softly. After a few moments NATALIA appears in the dining-room door. She is wearing an ill-fitting black dress and carrying a tray containing a plate and a glass of tea. She seems nervous and ill at ease.

NATALIA: I'm not disturbing you, am I?

ANTON: Of course not. (*Stops writing and takes off his pince-nez.*)

NATALIA: I've brought your food. You've hardly touched it. You left the table so suddenly. Can I put it here?

ANTON: Yes, that's fine.

ANTON moves aside some papers and NATALIA puts the tray down on the table.

NATALIA: You need to eat after your long journey. (*Short silence.*) I'm sure Aleksander didn't mean what he said to you. You know how…difficult he can be when he's drunk.

ANTON: (*Smiling.*) And sober.

NATALIA: Eat while it's still warm. Cold food tastes so horrible. (*Irritably.*) And you should open a window! (*She lights candles.*)

ANTON: The mosquitoes and the moths will come in. And the farm-cats. (*Suddenly becoming disarmingly playful and charming.*) While I was away a cat peed on one short story and half a vaudeville. Now cats are renowned for having extremely acute critical faculties. So, naturally I tore up all the pages and threw them away. If that sort of thing happens too often, I'm likely to become demoralized. (*Short silence.*) Don't you think?

NATALIA: (*Smiles. Nods. Suddenly weepy.*) I feel so tired. Quite dizzy. Would you mind…if I sat down for a little?

ANTON: By all means.

NATALIA sits. Short silence. NATALIA gives a little shuddering sigh.

NATALIA: He gets drunk almost every night now. He shouts and screams and frightens the boys. And I get such headaches...and palpitations. Really...my nerves can hardly stand it.

ANTON: You're too...refined dear Natalia. Always have been. You should be like me. I have no finer feelings at all. (*Silent laugh.*)

Short silence. ANTON looks down at his hands.

Has my mother gone to bed?

NATALIA: She wanted to wait for the old women from the village. I've just taken her up. She's still weeping and she won't undress.

ANTON: I can just see her. Lying on the counterpane wearing her stays, her dress and even those alarming little boots. By the way, which old women from the village?

NATALIA: The Lintvariovs sent them to keep a vigil all night. Professional mourners.

ANTON: (*Laughs.*) Oh, my God!

NATALIA: I asked if I could do anything for her... To make her more comfortable and she said all she wanted was Aleksander's boys to lie on either side of her. (*Sound of breaking crockery from the dining-room.*) Holy Mother of God! He's breaking things! (*Short silence. Tearful.*) I'm at my wits' end. I really am. (*Short silence.*) Poor retarded little boys. I try to be a mother to them.

Short silence. NATALIA pulls at her dress.

I must look so dreadful. I had to borrow this dress from the Lintvariovs. I never wear black, as you know. It's ugly. I shouldn't say that. They've really been very kind. And much too big for me. You know how slim I am. (*Pause. Gives a little laugh.*) Don't you remember how you used to call me 'my little skeleton'? (*Pause.*) Well... I've hardly put on any weight since then. In fact...I'm almost exactly the same. (*Short silence.*) I suppose I should go. You have work to do.

ANTON: (*Graciously.*) Not at all. Stay a bit and talk.

NATALIA: Thank you.

Short silence.

ANTON: I haven't even congratulated you properly. A married woman at last!

NATALIA: How can you say that to me? As if you don't know why I haven't married before.

ANTON: I'm sorry. I was only joking. I didn't mean anything by it.

NATALIA presses her palm over her eyes and starts crying softly.

Don't cry. Please. It makes you look too apallingly like that small carthorse. Do you remember it? The mangy one that used to eat your marigolds so sadly.

NATALIA gives a watery smile then she sighs.

NATALIA: You must wonder why I married him.

ANTON: It's obvious, isn't it? He's such a snappy dresser.

NATALIA: Oh, please be serious for once! Because you know how he treats me. You've seen for yourself. But... the fact is...he needs me. And those poor children need me. It's important for me to feel needed, you know. I feel at least that I have some reason...to go on.

ANTON: Yes. I understand.

NATALIA: And after…you stopped wanting me…for a long time I felt so somehow…useless. Just a poor, useless woman growing older every day. Staring at her own haggard face in the mirror.

Priest stops chanting.

ANTON: Thank God that's stopped. I couldn't bear it any longer.

Short silence.

NATALIA: I know I shouldn't speak like this. I'm embarrassing you. (*Gets up. Tearful.*) Really… It's unforgivable of me. Well…I'll go up to my room now. I'll go and pray for your poor brother's soul. (*Goes towards the door. Turns at the door.*) By the way, the Lintvariovs fetched Masha to spend the night with them. They're such good, kind people…

ALEKSANDER appears in the dining-room door. He looks dishevelled. He is unshaven and is wearing a crumpled shirt and pants that hang low on his hips. The bottle of vodka in his hand is half empty.

ALEKSANDER: Oh…there you are! (*Sways slightly. Silence.*) I think…you've been *avoiding* me.

ANTON: Why should you possibly think that? You're such scintillating company when you're drunk.

ALEKSANDER: But of course. (*Singing.*) 'Druuunk agaaain!! He's druuunk agaaain!' So tell me why?

ANTON: What are you talking about?

ALEKSANDER: Why are you *avoiding* me?

ANTON: I've told you, it's all in your mind.

ALEKSANDER: (*Shouting.*) You think I'm a fool? I know you Antosha. I…know…you…!

ANTON: I admit it. I admit it. I've been skulking and hiding. You see... (*Whimsical smile at NATALIA.*) I didn't want to be shown up in front of your new wife. When you're in such fine form...I become consumed with envy. How can I possibly compete with such brilliant repartee?

The eerie sound of wailing and keening women can be heard from the bedroom. The wailing continues throughout the scene. At times it is almost inaudible and at other times – as indicated in the text – the sound intensifies.

ALEKSANDER: (*Suddenly shouts.*) Shut up! Shut up! (*Wailing ceases.*) Have you seen those old women out there? Three old hags. (*Puts his lips over his teeth.*) Not a tooth between them. Stinking of cabbage! And fishy old cunt!

ANTON looks to NATALIA in apology.

NATALIA: It doesn't matter. I'm used to his foul language.

ALEKSANDER: Poor little woman. And married to such a brute. An animal.

NATALIA sighs. Short silence. Wailing tentatively resumes.

(*Mock animated. Throwing himself in a chair.*) So...tell me Antosha, did you have a good trip? What did you do on the country estate? Hunt? Eat gooseberries? Fuck virgins? I'm only asking because I'm interested. Lucky you. Lucky you. And poor us.

NATALIA: Aleksander, won't you please just go to bed. You're making everything much worse.

ALEKSANDER: (*To ANTON.*) Don't worry. I'm not going to say anything. I'm not...going to *accuse* you of...for instance...taking to your heels...leaving Kolia when he *needed* you the *most*. I won't say a *word* about that. When you *knew* he was dying. No...no...I *swear* I won't say *anything* about that. (*Claps his hand over his mouth.*)

NATALIA: Go to bed!

ALEKSANDER: *Neither* – mark my word – would I call you a *filthy coward.* No. I would *never* say anything like that to you. So you see…you needn't have…*avoided* me. (*Laugh.*) Please…please…don't take this personally… But I want to ask you a question. One…question. (*Drinks.*) Only…of course… (*Wipes his mouth on the back of his sleeve.*) If you don't mind.

ANTON: Ask me anything you want to.

ALEKSANDER: Only one, short question… (*Leans forward and peers at ANTON. Silence.*)

ANTON: (*Suddenly exploding.*) Well, for God's sake get on with it!

Silence while ALEKSANDER still peers at him.

ALEKSANDER: (*Whispering loudly.*) Where…were…you? (*Louder.*) Where…the fuck…*were* you!!

NATALIA: Don't you have any respect! (*Indicating the bedroom.*) Your brother is lying in there! Dead!

ALEKSANDER: Precisely. That's the point! And don't think I want to know! No! *He* (*Points to the bedroom.*) wants to know! He's asking, '*Where were you brother fucking doctor, when I was dying in fucking agony!*'

Short silence.

ANTON: (*Quietly.*) There weren't any gooseberries. There weren't any virgins. And we played lotto because it rained. (*Gets up. Goes to the window and looks out.*)

NATALIA: Aleksander, I beg you, if you have any feelings for me, then leave it. Please…everyone's so very tired. You need some sleep. Just go to bed.

Short silence. ALEKSANDER looks slightly dazed.

ALEKSANDER: You're right. Everyone is very tired. Of course. Very tired.

NATALIA: Come on then.

ALEKSANDER: Can I sleep with you?

NATALIA: (*Taking ALEKSANDER's arm.*) Masha's not here… and I have to sleep on the sofa in your mother's room. (*Leading him to the hall door.*) She's in a bad way.

ALEKSANDER: No…I'm not going to sleep alone! (*Pulls away from her and falls down on the bed.*) I'm sleeping here.

NATALIA: But that's Anton's bed.

ANTON: Let him sleep there if he wants to. I won't go to bed. I have a lot of work to do. (*Turning.*) I'll go and work in the dining-room. (*Goes towards the table.*)

NATALIA: If you're sure?

ANTON: Yes.

ALEKSANDER: And…what…is keeping you so busy?

NATALIA: He's writing. Can I help you?

ANTON: Thanks. If you can take the ink-well.

ALEKSANDER: Well…good for you. (*Kicks his shoe off. He kicks it high into the air and it falls heavily to the floor.*) Good for you! (*Does the same with the other shoe.*)

NATALIA follows ANTON to the dining-room.

(*Calling after ANTON.*) You don't let anything go to waste, do you! I admire that! I'm sure you can *squeeze* something out of this! A poignant, comic tale of pathetic, wasted lives!

Sound of ANTON and NATALIA speaking in low voices. ALEKSANDER sits up and tries to hear.

NATALIA: (*Entering.*) You must try and get some sleep now. (*Blows out a candle.*)

ALEKSANDER: Don't blow out the candles! I'm frightened of the dark!

NATALIA exits and closes the hall door behind her.

Don't close the door!

NATALIA opens the door and leaves. Silence. ALEKSANDER stares out in front of him. He lifts the vodka to his mouth and throws his head back.

(*Turns it upside down. Talking to himself.*) Not even a drop. What am I going to do? I can't be sober and live through this! I'll go stark, raving mad! In fact, I think I'm mad already. (*Loudly. Calling to ANTON.*) I think I've lost my mind!

ANTON: (*Off.*) What the hell's wrong now?

ALEKSANDER: I've run out of booze! Not a drop. (*To himself.*) I can't be without it tonight. (*To ANTON.*) I can't take it! You know what I'm like! Don't you have anything? Wine?

ANTON: No!

ALEKSANDER: Well... Surgical alcohol?

ANTON: Nothing!

ALEKSANDER: Cologne?

ANTON: (*Laugh.*) You're not drinking my cologne! It's imported!

ALEKSANDER: (*Talking to himself.*) There's that other half in the cubby-hole. Under the bed. But I can't go through there. It's just too hideous. With those wailing hags. Can't do it. Can't...bear to see him again. (*To ANTON.*) Why...don't you get it for me? Please Antosha! I never want to see that cubby-hole ever again in my life! That's where I was sleeping…last night when Kolia called me!

Short silence.

ANTON: (*Appears in the dining-room door with a pen in his hand.*) I slept there for two months before you came. Listening to his coughing. He used to wake me four or five times a night. I want you to know that! (*Exits.*)

ALEKSANDER: (*Calling after him.*) It's not the same! You can't even imagine what it was like!

Short silence.

Please Antosha…! Just get it for me! I need it desperately! It's a medical emergency. Please!

Short silence.

I'm begging you! (*Falls on his knees.*) I'm on my knees!

ANTON: (*Off.*) What the fuck are you talking about? I don't even know what you're talking about!

ALEKSANDER: The vodka…in the cubby-hole! I told you! Will you get it for me?

ANTON: (*Off.*) I'm busy. Get it yourself!

ALEKSANDER: (*Gets up. Goes to the dining-room door and leans in the doorway.*) You haven't seen him yet, have you?

ANTON: (*Off.*) No.

ALEKSANDER: Horrible as it is…it's much better to look. If you don't, it's going to haunt you.

ANTON: (*Off.*) I have work to do! Leave me alone!

ALEKSANDER: You're such a…mean…heartless…bastard! (*Turns back into the room and goes to the bedroom door. Hesitates. To himself.*) I…can't do it. I just can't do it.

ANTON: (*Enters with a bottle of wine.*) Here, have this!

ALEKSANDER: (*Takes the bottle.*) It's sweet and very weak. (*Holds it up to the light.*) And there's not much left.

ANTON: (*Tired.*) Well leave it then.

A knock at the hall door and almost immediately NATALIA appears in the door. She has papers in her hand.

NATALIA: (*Coldly.*) I think I should give you these. They're not mine to keep. (*She holds out the papers.*)

ANTON: (*Crossing the room.*) What are they? (*Taking the papers.*) Looks like…letters of some kind. Who wrote them?

NATALIA: Kolia. Don't you recognise his handwriting?

ANTON: Doesn't look like his handwriting. So…wildly written. So many words underlined. Exclamation marks everywhere. In some places the pen's gone right through the paper. When did he write this?

NATALIA: Yesterday afternoon.

ALEKSANDER: (*Surprised.*) Yesterday afternoon? (*To ANTON.*) That's when I went crayfishing.

ANTON: All these letters. It must have exhausted him. But where did he find the paper and the ink?

NATALIA: It's all my fault! You might as well blame me! I gave them to him. But if you'd seen how terrified he was. Like a trapped animal. And he begged me. (*Tearful.*) What was I supposed to do?

ANTON: No one is blaming you, Natalia.

NATALIA: He said he'd been dreaming about his birthplace.

ALEKSANDER: (*Sarcastic.*) Taganrog.

NATALIA: Yes. He said he needed to write to his family there.

ANTON: (*Reading.*) 'I must get back to Taganrog! To bathe in the warm, shallow sea. I'm in great danger here! The flies and the heat are killing me! 'Taganrog…' I can't make it out.

ALEKSANDER: Filthy…stinking…putrid sewer!

ANTON: 'I will get better there. I know that. Please believe me. It is a matter of life and death!!!' Three exclamation marks.

ALEKSANDER: I hate it! I'll never see it again! I hate every stone. Every particle of dust!

ANTON: (*Reading another letter.*) 'In exchange for the train-tickets from Kharkov we send you a portrait of a woman in oils, very well done…'

ALEKSANDER: (*To NATALIA.*) That must be the portrait he did of you. What did he call it? 'Poverty', 'Misery', 'Tragedy'?

ANTON: I will die in this hole. (*ANTON reads slowly and with difficulty.*) 'Help me…not to die…like a dog.'

NATALIA: (*Tearful.*) He asked me to post them for him. He kept asking me to promise on my life. He was so frightened and alone. My sister should have been with him. But no one wanted to give her a train-ticket!

ALEKSANDER: That's all we needed! That grotesque!!

NATALIA: How can you call her that? They loved each other… But how can I expect you to understand something like that?

ALEKSANDER: That swollen tick sucked the life out of him and that's the truth!

NATALIA: You're unspeakable. Unspeakable! (*Storms out through the hall door.*)

Short silence.

ANTON: What's wrong with you?

ALEKSANDER: Don't start preaching to me.

Short silence.

ANTON: (*Reading.*) 'I beg you. I implore you. If I die here, no one...will remember me. I am only a burden...to my family.'

Short silence. ANTON looks stricken. He suddenly crumples up the letters and throws them on the floor.

ALEKSANDER: What are you doing?

ANTON: They're of no use to anyone. The ravings of a dying man.

ALEKSANDER: That's Kolia you're talking about!

ANTON: (*Shouting.*) Spare me your maudlin sentimentality!

NATALIA: (*Appearing in the hall door.*) She was the only one who cared about him...supported him...when all of you treated him like dirt! Just remember that! (*Storms out.*)

ALEKSANDER: (*Shouting after her.*) A swollen tick!!

Silence. ALEKSANDER sinks down on the bed and holds his head.

ANTON: Why did you marry her? If you're always insulting her?

Short silence.

ALEKSANDER: When she came to...help us after my Anna died...I hardly noticed her. She's not my kind of woman. But she has a way of...growing on you.

Then she wouldn't sleep with me because she didn't (*Mimicking NATALIA.*) 'want to give birth to a poor little bastard'. So I went and bought one of those new things…condons or condoms.

ANTON: I've heard of them.

ALEKSANDER: My prick was so big that the thing just split. And so…all we could do was to get married.

ANTON: (*Matter of fact.*) You married because your prick was too big.

ALEKSANDER: (*Mock triumphant.*) Well! At least I've achieved one thing in my life! I'm the very first Russian who ever bought one.

ANTON: Is that true? (*Laugh.*)

ALEKSANDER: It was even in the paper: (*Making a formal announcement.*) 'It has been established that Aleksander Pavlovich Chekhov of St Petersburg address unknown is the first Russian citizen to have bought the new birth control device imported from France.'

They laugh.

(*Short silence.*) Tell me something…why are you always so sorry for her? (*Mock sympathetic voice.*) Do you still fancy her? Tell me! I don't mind.

ANTON: Of course not. I just can't bear it when you're so cruel and unfeeling.

ALEKSANDER: Cruel…and unfeeling? Strange…those words remind me of something. Now what could it be I wonder? No…don't tell me. (*Walks about, chanting.*) Cruel and unfeeling, cruel and unfeeling, cruel and unfeeling. I have it! One word for cruel and unfeeling! Ten across! (*Takes a deep breath.*) 'A-sonavabitch-doctor-who-leaves-his-dying-brother-without-camphor-without-morphine-without-a-single-damn-thing-to-ease-his-suffering!'

ANTON: For God's sake…! I needed to get away! I was going crazy, can't you understand that? I'd been here for two hellish months. Cooped up. Mama and Masha scuttling and weeping! Then hardly ever sleeping! I didn't know he was going to die!

ALEKSANDER: You're a doctor! You should know these things!

ANTON: For the rest of my life…I'll remember that ragged peasant from Mirgorod who brought me a sopping wet telegram that I could hardly read! (*Short silence. Passes his hand over his eyes.*) But I could make out…'Kolia' and 'dead'. (*Short silence.*) And the terrible journey! Jesus Christ! The grey skies. Galloping along that road with the endless, stunted trees! Waiting at Godforsaken stations for hours and hours!

Silence. Wailing stops.

(*Quietly.*) Because of all the hours waiting in the cold I have haemorrhoids, like a huge bunch of grapes sticking out of my arse!

ALEKSANDER: Since I can remember I've been hearing about your bowels. I remember you…sitting on your pot, calling to me: (*High voice.*) 'It's stuck, it's stuck. It can't come out. Help me!'

ANTON: Don't you think I remember! And your idea of help was to pinch my arse black and blue.

ALEKSANDER: At least that made the turd fly out! (*Laughs. Drinks. Pause.*)

ANTON: Do you think it was easy for me? At least you had each other, but when I heard I was completely alone! Desperately alone!

ALEKSANDER: 'You had each other.' (*Strange laugh.*) When
I asked baby brother Misha to help me after Kolia
died…he spat… (*Illustrates.*) in my face right there at the
bedside. Then he started ranting and raving, threatening
to shoot me.

ANTON: Why did he do that?

ALEKSANDER: God knows. And then…he stormed in with
a rifle and I had to jump through the window and run
away. I had to spend the night on the damp ground
under a hedge. I…ache all over. I'll probably die of
rheumatic fever. I'll never forgive him…as God is my
witness. I'll detest him forever! I need a drink. Jesus! I
need a drink. Please Antosha… Please. Get it for me!
It…won't be so bad. What you imagine…is always
much worse. Please! Otherwise I don't think I'll be able
to make it. I really can't take much more.

Short silence.

ANTON: Yes. I suppose I should go in and see him.

ALEKSANDER: It won't be so bad. I promise you.

Wailing resumes.

ANTON gets up.

(*Takes his arm and propels him to the bedroom door.*) You
don't have to look too carefully. Walk very quickly and
just glance at him out of the corner of your eye.

ANTON: Yes… (*Opens the door slightly.*)

ALEKSANDER: You'll be there and back in a minute. (*Giving
him a little push. Whisper.*) The vodka's in the pisspot.

*ANTON disappears into the bedroom and ALEKSANDER closes
the door securely behind him. Then he goes to the sofa and
throws himself down. He closes his eyes tightly. After a while
he starts singing quietly.*

'There was a pretty girl, who always wore a smock,
The only time she lifted it...'

*ANTON enters and closes the bedroom door behind him. He
is holding a half bottle of vodka. He looks ashen and shaky.
ANTON opens the vodka, sits down on a step and drinks deeply.
He stares out in front of him.*

ANTON: Why... (*Strange laugh.*) ...is he lying in a white
coffin lined with rose silk? (*Laugh.*) It's ridiculous.
(*Laugh.*) A coffin for a rich virgin. (*Laugh.*)

ALEKSANDER: The Lintvariovs said they'd pay. And so...I
chose the most expensive!

ANTON: (*Quietly. With extreme sadness.*) Kolia would have
loved it. He would have laughed...until he pissed
himself.

Silence.

*ANTON sits motionlessly, staring out in front of him.
ALEKSANDER watches him. ALEKSANDER gets up, crosses
and sits next to him on the step. ALEKSANDER takes the bottle
from him and drinks.*

ALEKSANDER: Can I ask you something, Antosha?

ANTON: Yes.

ALEKSANDER: Why don't you ever cry? You don't ever
cry...about him. I've never, ever seen you cry. When
father used to thrash us, Kolia and I would howl, but
you never shed a tear. Why Antosha?

Short silence.

ANTON: I don't know. (*Short silence.*) Maybe...I didn't want
to give him the satisfaction. I used to...clench my teeth
to stop myself.

ALEKSANDER: Yes, you never made a sound. It was terrible.

ANTON: And since then…it's as if I don't have any more tears. They just…won't come. (*Short laugh.*)

ALEKSANDER: Wicked old devil! How he mutilated us! (*Quietly.*) One day I'll kill him. (*He drinks.*) Well thank God at least he's back in Moscow. The old swine!

Silence as they sit deep in thought. They take turns to swig from the bottle.

Now the sound of one thin voice wailing plaintively. Silence as they listen.

Do you know what that reminds me of?

ANTON: No.

ALEKSANDER: Just listen.

ANTON listens.

ANTON: I can't remember.

ALEKSANDER: Close your eyes and listen.

ANTON closes his eyes.

I'll give you two words: 'Taganrog' and 'still-born'. (*Drinks.*)

Silence as ANTON listens intensely.

One more: 'Fur-coat'.

ANTON: (*Opening his eyes.*) Of course! My God, how could I forget! That man, what was his name? Something with an M. Sounded like Mozarov.

ALEKSANDER: Something like that.

ANTON: He always wore a fur-coat even in summer.

ALEXANDER laughs.

And that shy, furtive little wife of his had a still-birth every year. They lived just behind us.

ALEKSANDER: And each time it happened she used to wail, for days and days.

ANTON: Yes! Of course! (*Takes the bottle from ALEKSANDER and drinks.*) All buried in the backyard. Just weeds and (*Gesture.*) rows and rows of small white crosses.

Silence as they listen to the wailing.

ALEKSANDER: (*Puts his head in his hands. Mutters.*) Oh God... Oh God... Oh God.

Sound of a distant shot.

ANTON: What the hell is that?

ALEKSANDER stops weeping and listens. Another shot. ALEKSANDER looks at the window. He gets up, crosses to the window and opens it.

ALEKSANDER: (*Calling loudly.*) Misha! You bastard! Are you out there?! Do you still want to shoot me? You snivelling little weasel! Show yourself and be a man for once! Here I am! Do it now! Do it now!!! Noow!!! Noow!! (*Tearful.*) Now... Do it...now. (*Weeps. Sinks slowly to the floor and lies sobbing in a crumpled heap with his head pressed to the wall.*)

Silence. They listen to the wailing. It grows softer, sounding more like keening.

ALEKSANDER looks up at ANTON. His face is contorted with grief.

(*Falteringly.*) I... I...can't... (*Makes repetitive hand gesture.*) stop...seeing... (*He gasps as if he has difficulty breathing.*) Over...and over...

ANTON: It must have been...unspeakable.

ALEKSANDER nods. His face is still contorted with pain.

ALEKSANDER: Oh, God... (*Falters. Sits up with his back against the wall and his legs drawn up.*) When I lifted him onto the pot...he was so light...I could... (*Faltering.*) I could...feel every bone under his skin...

Short silence.

I don't want to...talk about it...think about it... You don't know what it was like when the breathing stopped...and it was suddenly so quiet.

Short silence.

ANTON: I'm sorry you had to be alone. (*Quietly. Bitter.*) I...should have been here. I'll always blame myself.

ALEKSANDER: You said you didn't know. (*Short silence.*) I believe you. It's not your fault. I'm sorry...I was so fucked up.

Short silence.

ANTON: I don't think you *should* believe me.

ALEKSANDER: What do you mean?

ANTON: I think I might have lied to you. In some...deep way...I probably knew. In fact...I'm almost sure I did. I knew. And that's the truth.

ALEKSANDER: You bastard! You filthy, cowardly bastard! How could you *do* that? How could you *do* that to him? (*Crawls to ANTON. He grabs him by his shoulders and starts shaking him and pushing him around.*) You disgusting... filthy...coward!

ALEKSANDER loses his balance. He falls down and pulls anton with him.

ANTON: (*On the floor.*) For God's sake! (*Starts laughing.*)

ALEKSANDER: (*Blind with rage and pounding ANTON with his fists.*) Damn you! Stop laughing! Stop it! (*Grabs ANTON by the hair and bangs his head against the floor.*)

ANTON: (*Covering his face with his arms.*) No! (*Laughs.*) This is absurd!

ALEKSANDER: I'll kill you!…I swear…I'll…kill you! You… disgusting…piece of shit!!

ANTON: (*Catches ALEKSANDER by the wrists.*) You don't have to kill me. (*Laughs.*) I'm half dead already! (*Laughs.*) You can save yourself the trouble!

They look at each other for a moment, then ANTON lets go of ALEKSANDER's wrists and turns his face away.

ALEKSANDER: You talk such shit!

ANTON: (*Wiping away the tears of laughter.*) I also have it. The family curse. The raging bacilli. Sometimes… I almost hear them…multiplying…multiplying in my blood… Consuming me.

ALEKSANDER: You're lying to me aren't you? You're lying to me!!

ANTON: It's true, damn you!!

Short silence.

Seeing him…seeing him die…would have been like… seeing myself.

ALEKSANDER: My God. (*Pause.*) I can't believe it. (*Gets up slowly.*)

ANTON: (*Sitting up slowly.*) I've been spitting blood for years. I've always had fevers, even as a child. It's different with strangers or patients. But with Kolia…it would have been like seeing…everything. Every moment of…what I'll be suffering. (*Short silence.*) It's selfish, I know. And cowardly. You're right about that. (*Gets up.*)

ALEKSANDER: You've never looked better in your life! And…and there are new treatments. Vasily was just skin and bone. He drank mare's milk and now he's as fat as a pig! You're a doctor… There are things you can do! (*Short silence.*) Why did you never tell me? But then I'm just 'Aleksander the hack'. 'Aleksander the muck-mouth.'

ANTON: (*Quietly.*) I've hardly…told myself.

ALEKSANDER: I'm sure it's not that bad. You'll probably outlive me by twenty years. I'll never get rid of you. I mean, that would be too good to be true. (*Laugh.*)

ANTON: You're right. (*Wry.*) I'll live until I'm a hundred and five. I'll have endless fat wives. I'll populate the earth with raving Chekhovs.

Short silence.

ALEKSANDER: You're not really dying are you?

ANTON: (*Pause.*) Of course not.

ALEKSANDER: You're such a liar. (*Short silence.*) And to think I almost believed you. I'm a bloody fool. (*Short silence.*) Aren't I a bloody fool? There's nothing wrong with you.

ANTON: Nothing.

Short silence. Wailing intensifies.

ALEKSANDER: (*With quiet despair.*) Oh God… God…why can't they just…shut up?

Silence.

ANTON: You should really try and get some sleep. Tomorrow's going to be hell.

ALEKSANDER: I know.

Short silence.

ANTON: Do you know what the worst part of it is for me? Carrying the coffin. Feeling the weight of that...thing that isn't really Kolia any more.

ALEKSANDER: I know.

ANTON: I suppose our mother and Masha will be sobbing their eyes out. I'm sure. The usual display. (*Short silence.*) I must try not to think about that. Get some sleep.

ALEKSANDER: Yes.

ANTON gets up to leave.

No... Please... Don't go. Please just sit here for a while. Until I drop off.

Short silence.

I wish you could tell me a story as you used to.

ANTON: (*Sitting again.*) I don't have any more happy stories to tell.

Short silence.

ALEKSANDER: (*Plumping his pillow.*) The fleas are terrible in this place.

ANTON: Fleas...mosquitoes...flies...mould. Summer in the Russian country.

ALEKSANDER settles down and pulls the blanket up to his nose.

ALEKSANDER: I don't think I'll be able to sleep. And I think I'm breaking out in hives.

ANTON: Goodnight Aleksander. (*Blows out candle.*)

Silence.

ALEKSANDER: And I think I'm getting a fever. (*Puts his hand on his forehead.*) In fact... I'm burning up. Come and feel. Just come and feel.

ANTON crosses to him and puts his hand on his forehead.

What do you think?

ANTON: You won't last the night. We'll have a double funeral.

ALEKSANDER: Oh, you're such a bloody quack. And I'm dying of thirst. (*Points at the carafe and glass on the table.*) Is there water in that carafe?

ANTON: Yes.

ALEKSANDER: Pour me some, won't you.

ANTON pours water into the glass.

Do you think it's been boiled? I don't want to die of cholera. Everyone shits in the river.

ANTON gives him the glass of water.

It's as yellow as piss. (*Takes a sip.*) And there's a bloody monstrous cockroach in it! (*Fishes it out.*)

ANTON: (*Laugh.*) Oh, for God's sake, go to sleep.

ALEKSANDER: I want to...but I'm too scared. I might as well tell you that nothing's changed. Every night Kolia and I would be shitting ourselves. We were so fucking terrified of having bad dreams.

Silence. ANTON goes to the window and looks out.

ANTON: (*Quietly.*) The three of us sleeping in the same bed for all those years. That...old...hollow...feather-bed. You or Kolia used to wet the bed almost every night!

ALEKSANDER: (*Laugh.*) Sometimes both of us!

ANTON: God, half my childhood was spent sleeping in that tangled, dank, stinking heap.

ALEKSANDER: (*Almost sadly.*) Of course, you never pissed in the bed. You were never scared. Brave little brother Anton. Telling us stories to put us to sleep. (*To himself.*) I've never stopped having nightmares. Sometimes I think I go straight to hell every night. Won't you come and sit with me. Just for a bit. Please.

ALEKSANDER suddenly starts sobbing into his pillow.

ANTON: What's wrong now?

ALEKSANDER: (*Tearful.*) I keep thinking of all the times I treated him so badly. When we lived together I used to swear and shout at him for having filthy feet...for slopping paint everywhere...for snoring like a hog. Once...I even threw him out in the middle of a cold night. I'm sorry Kolia. I'm sorry, I'm sorry.

ANTON: Don't torture yourself.

ALEKSANDER: Why wasn't I nicer to him? Why did I always shit on his head like that?

ANTON: It's all in the past. You must forget about it.

Short silence.

ALEKSANDER: Do you think...he's forgiven me?

ANTON: Of course. Of course he has. At least he didn't die alone. At least you were with him at the end. Just remember that.

Short silence.

Maybe he's looking down at you. Maybe he's thinking: 'There's Aleksander. What an excuse for a brother. Still too scared to blow out the candle. Still hiding under his blanket. Drunk again…with borscht in his hair. But…at least… (*Pauses significantly.*) he got…one…thing…right.'

ALEKSANDER chuckles sleepily.

(*Quietly.*) One thing. One…thing.

Silence. The wailing can still be heard, but now more faintly. ANTON sits staring out front. The lights slowly fade to black.

ACT TWO

Dim light. Only the lamp on the table is burning. ALEKSANDER is asleep on the bed. He is snoring softly. Dim light can be seen through the half-open study door.

A soft knock on the hall door. Short silence. The knock is repeated. Then the door is opened very quietly. NATALIA peers around the door. She sees ALEKSANDER asleep on the bed. Then she looks towards the study. She enters stealthily. She is wearing a white cotton nightdress and her hair is loose. She crosses to the study and knocks tentatively on the open door.

NATALIA: (*Calling softly.*) Anton.

ANTON: (*Off.*) What's wrong?

NATALIA: (*Loud whisper.*) It's your mother. I just thought... I should come and tell you.

ANTON comes to the door.

ANTON: (*Speaking quietly.*) What's wrong with her? I thought she was asleep.

NATALIA: (*Loud whisper.*) Yes...yes, she is. But she's growing very restless. I'm afraid those poor boys are disturbing her. I can't get them to be still, you see. I...
I don't know what to do.

ANTON: (*Quietly.*) Do you think they should sleep somewhere else?

NATALIA: (*Loud whisper.*) Yes. Well...possibly. (*Glances at ALEKSANDER.*) I don't want to wake him. Poor thing. Don't you think we should speak...in there.

ALEKSANDER wakes up.

ANTON: Yes...yes, of course. Why don't you come in?

NATALIA goes into the study.

ALEKSANDER: (*Sitting up.*) What's happening?

NATALIA: (*Entering from the study.*) I just came to tell you that your mother is… Well, that she's rather restless. You were asleep…so I've been telling Anton.

Short silence.

ALEKSANDER: Is that so? Are you quite sure that it's our mother that's 'restless'? Are you quite sure of that?

NATALIA: I don't know what you mean?

ALEKSANDER: Come here. Come closer. I want to look at you.

Short silence. NATALIA approaches ALEKSANDER unwillingly.

ANTON: Well, I suppose I'd better go and see her. (*Crosses quickly to the hall door and exits.*)

NATALIA: Why are you looking at me like that?

ALEKSANDER: I'm looking. Just looking.

Short silence.

NATALIA: Well…that's all I came to say. (*Turns to go.*)

ALEKSANDER: Wait a minute. What are you doing?

NATALIA: What do you mean?

ALEKSANDER: Dressed like that! I can see everything! (*Gets up and approaches her.*) And the hair! (*Lifts a strand of hair.*) Brushed and shining!

NATALIA: I was just going to bed.

ALEKSANDER: Oh? Is that so? (*Sniffs.*) You don't go to bed smelling like this! Perfumed like a Babylonian whore!

NATALIA gives a little gasp and turns to go. ALEKSANDER grabs her arm.

Come here! Let me look at you.

NATALIA turns her face away.

I want to see what a woman looks like who's been praying day and night – isn't that what you said? – for my brother's soul. Look at me! (*Grabs her by the hair and turns her face to him.*) What do I see?

She gives a cry.

Is that rouge I see? (*Wipes his cuff over her cheek.*)

ANTON: (*Entering from the dining-room.*) What the hell is going on? What are you doing?

ALEKSANDER: Look at that? (*Shows ANTON his cuff.*) Look! Rouge! She's painted and powdered and perfumed herself like a whore! (*To NATALIA.*) Do you think I'm stupid? Do you think I'm a fucking fool? Look at her! Wearing that thin thing! Nothing underneath!

ANTON: What are you talking about?

NATALIA weeps quietly.

ALEKSANDER: Can't you see? Can't...you...see? It wasn't about our mother. She didn't want to tell us anything! No! She thought I'd be fast asleep! Drunk, passed out, dead-to-the-world. Tip-toeing (*Tip-toes grotesquely.*) down here like a bitch on heat!

NATALIA gives a cry and runs out to the hall. Short silence.

ANTON: Does it please you...to humiliate that woman in front of me? (*Short silence.*) Does it make you feel important?

Short silence.

ALEKSANDER: Do you know what it feels like… (*Becoming weepy.*) to be married to a…strumpet… To a strumpet? (*Weeps quietly and drunkenly.*)

ANTON: My God… You're a misery.

ALEKSANDER: Why don't you go and…comfort her? Why don't you go and…give it to her?! (*Drinks deeply. Mutters.*) Slut…bitch…whore…cunt…

A knock at the bedroom door. Another knock. ANTON crosses to the bedroom door.

God! Don't open it! We mustn't open that door.

ANTON: Don't be ridiculous.

ALEKSANDER: What if it's him? Wanting to get in. Staring at us with his dead eyes!

ANTON: Just stay calm. (*Moves to the bedroom door.*)

ALEKSANDER: Don't! (*Covers his eyes.*)

ANTON opens the door. Sound of a deep voice muttering something.

ANTON: (*Turns his head to ALEKSANDER.*) It's the priest. He says he's been called away, but he'll be back in time for the funeral. (*To priest.*) Of course. Of course. (*Closes the door.*)

ALEKSANDER: (*Mutters.*) I wipe my arse on your beard Father.

ANTON: That was the one who gave Kolia 'absolution'.

ALEKSANDER: I just can't believe it. You know how he hated priests. Called them 'pisspots' and 'dog-turds'.

ANTON recounts the tale of Kostia's 'absolution' in a still, quiet way. As if the memory of that occasion is deeply painful to him.

ANTON: He was terrified. You should have seen him. He might have lived another few weeks, but the shock killed him. That's what I think.

ALEKSANDER: Why did you bring him here? Why didn't you stop her?

ANTON: I tried to. But she kept weeping and saying (*Mimicking mother.*) 'I don't want my son to go to hell. I don't want my son to go to hell.' She wore me down! You know what she's like.

ALEKSANDER: (*Mutters.*) Old cow!

ANTON: When he woke up that apparition was standing next to his bed with his long beard touching the sheets. Kolia started weeping and asking if he was going to die. (*Sits down on the foot of the bed.*) The Priest started making signs...chanting and singing in Greek. I was so bloody angry, but I couldn't do anything. Then he started blubbering...and crying...and confessing.

ALEKSANDER: What did he say?

ANTON: (*Gently mimicking Kolia.*) 'I've been a drunkard... I've blasphemed...I've treated my mother badly.'

ALEKSANDER: That must have pleased her.

ANTON: Oh, it did. (*Mimicking mother.*) 'He's saved, God be praised.'

ALEKSANDER: (*Mutters.*) I could kill her!

ANTON: (*Mimicking Kolia.*) 'I've always had filthy and lustful thoughts. I've fornicated with fat Anna.' (*Mimicking priest.*) 'How often, my son? (*Mimicking Kolia.*) 'A few thousand times.'

ALEKSANDER: He said that? In front of mother?

ANTON: Yes.

ALEKSANDER chuckles.

(*Quietly.*) And while the priest was making the sign of the cross, Kolia suddenly sat forward…and blood started gushing out.

ALEKSANDER: God.

ANTON: Mother said, 'Please God, take him now. Now… when he's been washed clean of his sins.' I could have strangled her with my bare hands. (*Short silence.*) And all the time I was thinking of how much that old priest reminds me of our father who art in Moscow. The same sour smell of piety.

ALEKSANDER: It makes me sick to the stomach.

Short silence.

My God…poor Kolia. Poor bastard. Maybe I'll be the same. Maybe I'll shit in my pants when my time comes.

Short silence.

ANTON: Christ, what a strange world we grew up in. Filled with demons and saints and angels. And just waiting for us all… (*Deep voice.*) 'the yawning pit of hell'.

ALEKSANDER: No wonder I still dream of ghouls and spectres. (*Yawns.*)

ANTON: I used to think God lived in Taganrog church. And because there were icon lamps, I used to think God had many red, yellow and green eyes. (*Pause.*) When I have a child, I'll protect him from such horror. I'll protect him with my life.

Sound of wailing intensifies.

ALEKSANDER: Jesus…just listen to them. I can't take it any more. (*Shouts loudly.*) Can't they just shut up, for God's sake! Disgusting old hags!

The wailing intensifies almost unbearably.

(*Shouts.*) Carrion crows!!

ANTON laughs.

ANTON: Vultures!! Harpies!! (*Laughs.*)

ALEKSANDER: Scavengers!! Shut up!! (*Rushes towards the bedroom door. Flings open the door.*) Shut up and fuck off!! (*Off.*) Get out or I'll wring your scrawny necks!! Moulting old hens!!

Cacophony of high-pitched screams and ALEKSANDER shouting 'Get out!!' while ANTON is depressed, staring at the floor. The screams and ALEKSANDER's shouts of 'Get out!!' etc. recede slowly into the distance. He looks at the open bedroom floor. As he crosses to the bedroom the sound of muffled sobbing is heard from upstairs and, seconds later, hurried footsteps on the stairs.

ANTON: Oh God…

Footsteps in the hall. NATALIA appears in the doorway. She looks dishevelled.

NATALIA: All that noise has woken up your mother! She's sobbing and moaning and tearing her hair out! Please, you must come and help!

ANTON: Christ! I'll have to give her something. Where… did I put my bag?

The sound of glass breaking upstairs. Also the continued sound of muffled sobbing.

Please go up and see what's happening.

NATALIA exits. Sounds of her hurried footsteps receding, then going up the stairs. ANTON finds his doctor's bag. He puts it on the table and starts rummaging through it. After a few moments ALEKSANDER's *footsteps can be heard in the bedroom. He appears in the door.*

ALEKSANDER: (*Breathless.*) At least I got rid of them. (*Laugh. Closes the door behind him.*)

Muffled sobbing can still be heard from upstairs.

What's that? (*Listens.*) What's that sound?

ANTON: It's mother. I'll have to give her an injection.

ALEKSANDER: Oh, Jesus! (*Puts his hands over his ears.*)

ANTON: (*Taking out a syringe.*) If I can find another needle. This one is bent.

ALEKSANDER: (*With his hands still over his ears.*) She cried like that...do you remember? For weeks...and weeks... when our little sister died. Oh, God...the same sound.

ANTON: (*Rummaging in his bag.*) Where the bloody hell is it?

ALEKSANDER: (*Takes his hands away from his ears.*) We were so terrified at night...we thought she'd come and haunt us with...her pale little face. (*Listens.*) Why does she cry...in that horrible way? It doesn't even sound human!

ANTON: (*Finding a needle.*) Thank God! (*Putting the needle in the syringe.*)

Sound of NATALIA's *hurried footsteps on the stairs.*

ALEKSANDER: (*Puts his hands over his ears.*) I don't want to hear it, I don't want to hear it. (*Hums so as not to hear.*)

NATALIA *appears in the hall door.*

NATALIA: It was only a glass that broke! But please come quickly...she's in a very bad way. She's torn off all her buttons!

ANTON: (*Picking up his doctors bag.*) Bring some boiling water. (*Exits hurriedly.*)

NATALIA: Yes… (*Follows him.*)

ALEKSANDER: (*Calling.*) Natalia! Natalia! Please! (*Goes to the hall door.*) I need to talk to you! (*Going into the hall. Off.*) Please listen to me. Just for a moment. Won't you please just come in here?

NATALIA: (*Off.*) Say what you want to say! I'm in a hurry!

ALEKSANDER: (*Off.*) I can't bear that sobbing. (*Enters.*) Won't you come in here?

NATALIA: (*Pushing past him.*) I only have a minute.

ALEKSANDER closes the hall door.

Short silence.

ALEKSANDER: (*Tearful.*) Please… Please…will you forgive me? I'm sorry. I…despise myself. It's just…that I'm not myself. I…hardly even know…what I'm doing. I'm so shocked. (*Tearful.*) You don't know what it's like to lose a brother. To…be torn apart by this unbearable grief. (*Tearful.*) I don't deserve you… I know it. I don't. You're a wonderful woman. Only I know how wonderful. Please…just say you forgive me.

NATALIA: (*Coldly.*) I forgive you. Can I go now?

ALEKSANDER: But…I want you to mean it. Please…won't you let me hold you?

NATALIA turns to go.

Just for a second…

NATALIA turns and stands motionless. ALEKSANDER goes to her, puts his arm around her and holds her against him.

Poor little Natalia… You're so cold… Poor little cold
Natalia… Never mind… I'll make you warm. (*Strokes her
back. Kisses her in her neck and then strokes her buttocks.*)

NATALIA: (*Pushing him away violently.*) Don't you have any
shame? I've been crying all night and praying for your
brother's soul. And in there… (*Points.*) your brother is
lying in his coffin!

ALEKSANDER: I know that!

NATALIA: And how can you touch me…when you reek of
alcohol and stale sweat!

ANTON: (*Off. Calling desperately.*) I need that water!

NATALIA: I'm coming, Antoshevu! I'm coming!

ALEKSANDER: Why do you call him that? I didn't know
you still called him that. Why do you call him that?
(*Grabs her arm. Hissing.*) Do you want me to smell like
him? To smell of imported cologne? You two-faced,
lying whore! Don't you think I know you? You're
not…disgusted because of poor Kolia! No! Brother
Anton, isn't it? How can I dare to lay my filthy paws on
you…when he's so close. I see how you look at him! I
can almost hear you panting!

NATALIA: (*Tearful.*) That's not true.

ALEKSANDER: Do you think I'm a fool? You're so bloody
pathetic. Don't you have any pride? Do you think he'll
ever look at you again? Even when you were younger…
he sloughed you off! He's finished with you! You poor,
miserable thing. Once I found one of those pleading,
desperate letters you wrote him. 'Darling Antoshevu,
Please reply to this I beg you. I include stamps.' (*Repeat.*)
I…include…stamps!

NATALIA: (*In tears.*) You're such a bastard.

ALEKSANDER: Sending him stamps! My Christ! And then you still salivate at the sight of him! How do you think that makes me feel?

NATALIA is crying quietly and brokenly.

ANTON: (*Voice off.*) Natalia! For God's sake!

NATALIA: I'm coming! (*Runs out to the hall.*)

ALEKSANDER: (*Grabs his head.*) Jeeesus! Jeeesus! (*Sits on the bed, with his head still in his hands.*)

Silence. The sound of sobbing has intensified. ANTON's voice can be heard very softly and indistinctly. Mother's high-pitched scream. Then the sound of NATALIA's hurried footsteps, going down the passage.

(*High voice. Mimicking NATALIA.*) 'I'm coming, Antoshevu… I'm coming Antoshevu!' (*Gets up.*) My life is a living hell!

Silence. The sound of sobbing has ceased.

(*Wrapping his arms around himself and moving about restlessly.*) I…might as well be dead. I wouldn't be surprised…if I go blind again. No. It wouldn't surprise me.

Sound of footsteps descending the stairs.

ANTON: (*Voice off.*) Be quick with that water!

ANTON's footsteps can be heard in the hall.

(*Entering.*) I need some morphine. She knocked the phial out of my hand. My God, what an ordeal! I should never have become a doctor! (*Rummaging in his bag.*) I should have become a rat-catcher! And poor Natalia is in tears again.

ALEKSANDER: (*Sarcastic.*) 'Poor Natalia, Poor Natalia.' You don't understand anything, do you? Always, 'What have you done to Poor Natalia?' 'How badly you treat Poor Natalia!' Always...preaching to me.

ANTON: Will you shut up! Why don't you help, instead of spewing this drivel!

ALEKSANDER: Always protecting her. That letter you wrote me, do you remember? After you visited us the last time. She got hold of it and she's clutched it to her bony bosom ever since! And if I do something she doesn't like...she follows me even into the earth-closet reading that letter...over and over again!

NATALIA: (*Appearing in the hall door.*) I have the boiling water.

ALEKSANDER: My God, I know it by heart! (*Mimicking NATALIA.*) 'No decent man would talk coarsely to a woman about shitting...about lavatory paper...walk around in front of the chamber maid without his trousers...shouting at the top of his voice! Katka! Bring the pisspot!'

ANTON and NATALIA exit.

ANTON: (*As he exits.*) But it's true! You're disgusting! You're a pig!

Sound of sobbing still continues. ANTON and NATALIA's hurried footsteps can be heard going up the stairs.

ALEKSANDER: (*Shouting after them. Still mimicking NATALIA.*) You're so fucking self-righteous! (*To himself.*) I might be a crude pig. Yes...I probably am a crude pig. (*Rushes into the hall. Off. Calling up the stairs.*) I fart! I burp! I swear and curse! But what right do you have to pass judgment on me? What right?!!

Sound of door being slammed upstairs.

(*Shouting loudly.*) I haven't behaved like a fucking bastard!!

A repetitive knock at the bedroom door. ALEKSANDER appears in the hall door looking alarmed. He stares at the bedroom door for a few seconds, then approaches the door and opens it cautiously.

You filthy old hag! Didn't I tell you to get out?

Sound of a whining voice.

I'll give you your five kopeks! I'll give them to you! (*Turns away from the door and starts looking for money. Muttering.*) I'll give you your blood-money, you old hag. (*Has a thought and rushes into the hall shouting. Off.*) She's my wife! It's got nothing to do with you!! Do you hear me!! (*Enters and starts looking around.*)

Sound of whining.

(*Looking through ANTON's jacket pockets.*) Stop that filthy whining! (*Finding money.*) Here. (*Goes to the door.*) Three kopeks! You can get the other tomorrow!

Whining voice.

Just shut up or you'll get nothing! (*Closes the bedroom door.*) What a repulsive creature. My God, I don't think I've ever seen a more repulsive creature in my life. (*Sinks down onto the bed.*)

ANTON's footsteps approaching.

ANTON: (*Off.*) Please bring me a glass of water. (*Enters and is carrying a syringe and a bottle of spirits.*) What the hell's the matter with you? Instead of helping, all you can do is to rave and rant like a lunatic! (*Goes to his doctor's bag.*)

ALEKSANDER: I just want you to stop judging me! Accusing me! Writing me filthy letters! Who are you to call me a brute? You screwed her brains out for as long as you wanted to and then you just got rid of her!

49

ANTON: (*Putting the syringe and the spirits in the doctor's bag.*) Why must you talk about this now?

ALEKSANDER: She's so tender-hearted... (*Tearful.*) You've never understood...how tender-hearted she is.

Short silence.

Unseen by ANTON or ALEKSANDER, NATALIA has appeared in the hall door. She stands motionless, watching them. She has a glass of water in her hand.

Do you...do you know what it's like to be married to a woman who only stays with you...so that she can be close to your brother?!

ANTON: That's nonsense. (*Closing the doctor's bag.*)

ALEKSANDER: And because it gives her an excuse to hang your portrait on the wall. To say your name every day. And the way she croons your name. 'Antooon.' Once she even called it out in bed while I was poking her! (*Mimicking.*) 'An-to-she-vu!'

They both become aware of NATALIA standing in the doorway. She enters briskly and puts the glass of water on the table.

ANTON: I've just been telling Aleksander that we had a hellish time up there and that he made it ten times worse. (*Opens the doctor's bag.*)

NATALIA: Yes. That's true. But then...he's never been very considerate.

ALEKSANDER: Unlike my perfect brother.

ANTON: You can't even imagine what it was like! She was writhing and thrashing about. Natalia had to hold her down...and then I had to jab a needle into her! Jesus, what an ordeal! (*Takes out a glass bottle containing pinkish powder. Opens it. Tries to measure out some powder but his hand shakes. To NATALIA.*) Can you help me to measure this out? Please. My hand isn't steady.

NATALIA takes the spoon from him.

Just a quarter of a teaspoon in the water.

NATALIA: (*Reading the label.*) 'Opium in Aromatic Chalk.'

ANTON: I need something. Jesus. I could hardly inject her. I could hardly hold the syringe.

NATALIA: Is that right?

ANTON: Yes. Maybe a little more. Shrieking and thrashing and looking at me. Accusing me. God knows for what.

NATALIA stirs the powder into the water and gives it to him.

Thank you. (*Drinks.*) Then having to lift up her dress and all those petticoats. And that smell in the room. Camphor. But something else too. Something putrid. (*Shudders. To NATALIA.*) Would you put that back please? And close the bag.

NATALIA puts the bottle back and closes the bag.

ALEKSANDER: Why don't you give me something? You can see what a state I'm in.

ANTON: You've had too much to drink.

ALEKSANDER: I suppose you don't want to waste your precious medicine on me. Pretending to be generous. But you're actually cheap. Do you know that?

NATALIA: Why must you always criticize your brother? Can't you see how pale he is? And shaking like a leaf. You only think about yourself. Can't you consider someone else for once?

ALEKSANDER: You mean…be as considerate as my brother?

NATALIA: Yes. Anton can be so good and kind. You should have seen how gentle he was to your mother.

ALEKSANDER: The soul of kindness, that's true. A real gentleman. Look how kind he was to you. And to all… the other ladies. So great is his kindness! So universally admired! That it's…celebrated in song! Men sing it in Taverns! Raise their voices and sing about him!

As ANTON continues to speak, ALEKSANDER sings while ANTON interjects. Together:

ANTON: Oh, for God's sake…

ALEKSANDER: (*Sings.*) 'Keep your wives and virgins…'

ANTON: Won't you just shut up!

ALEKSANDER: (*Sings.*) 'Under key and lock…'

ANTON: Just for once in your miserable life!

ALEKSANDER: (*Sings.*) 'Under key and loooock…!'

ANTON: Everyone's heard it. Everyone's bored to death with it!

ALEKSANDER: But she hasn't has she? (*To NATALIA.*) You haven't, have you? Well…then it's going to be a nice surprise. (*Jumps on the table.*) A little…light relief.

(*Sings grotesquely.*)
'Keep your wives and virgins
Under key and lock
Under key and loooock!
Here comes Doctor Chekhov
With his swollen cock
With his swoooollen…'

NATALIA turns and moves rapidly to the hall door.

And do you know what it means?

NATALIA stops at the door.

That he's a cold-blooded, dirty, cheap philanderer! Everybody knows it! Everybody except you! That's how 'kind' he is! At least he only broke your heart. At least he didn't drive you insane, like poor Olga Kudosova!

ANTON: You're a liar! I didn't drive her crazy! She's always been strange and you know it!

ALEKSANDER: Since you finished with her, she's not just strange! She's raving mad and locked up in an asylum! You bastard! Deflowering virgins! Seducing other men's wives!

NATALIA: I won't hear any more! (*To ALEKSANDER.*) You're such an ingrate! You know how much he's done for you. You don't know him. You don't know him as I do.

ALEKSANDER: Excuse me, Madam. Of course not. What was I thinking of? You'll never see the truth will you? Well...think what you like! I don't care any more! I don't care! I'm sick of it! I've had it...with both of you! I'm finished with you!! Finished!! For all I care, you can both go to hell!! (*Storms out to the hall.*)

A silence. NATALIA and ANTON look shocked. The sound of the front door being slammed.

ANTON: Why don't you go after him?

NATALIA: Please...don't ask me to do that.

ANTON: You saw what he's like. God knows what he's capable of in this state.

NATALIA: I'm sorry... (*Tearful.*) I just can't any more. I just don't understand. (*Sigh.*) I don't understand people like him.

A slight noise upstairs.

ANTON: Did you hear that? (*Listens.*) Do you think she's asleep?

NATALIA: I hope so.

ANTON goes to the hall door and listens. NATALIA tidies loose strands of hair and smooths her nightgown.

ANTON: (*Turning back.*) I don't hear anything. It must be the rats. Well, thank God for that. (*Pause.*) Now I can get on with my work.

NATALIA: What are you working on at the moment? You don't have to talk about it if you don't want to. I remember a time…when I always knew precisely. And everyone envied me.

ANTON: (*In a tired way.*) I'm writing a story about a man called Gusev. He's a consumptive soldier who's being sent home from China in a rusty old steam ship. It's sweltering and very cramped. He's feverish and constantly hallucinating. Anyway, he dies, they wrap him in a winding sheet and throw him overboard. He sinks down…down…until he comes to rest at the bottom. I haven't quite finished it yet. I'm still looking for an ending.

NATALIA: Poor Gusev. (*Little laugh.*) We used to talk about your work sometimes all night. (*Little laugh.*) At times you even took my advice.

ANTON: I remember.

Awkward silence.

NATALIA: I overheard what Aleksander said. About why I married him. (*Pause.*) Did you believe him?

ANTON: Of course not.

NATALIA: I see.

ANTON: It's been years now. That's all in the past.

NATALIA: Yes, of course. You're right. All in the past. All...gone and forgotten.

Silence. NATALIA goes to the window and looks out. She gives a stifled sob.

ANTON: God, I'm tired. I need to sleep.

NATALIA: Sometimes...my life now...seems to be a strange, unhappy dream. Those...dark, crowded little rooms we live in... Aleksander getting drunk and cursing... And then of course those retarded little boys. (*Tearful.*) Really...I don't quite know how it happened.

Short silence.

Tell me...do you ever think about the years we spent together? Or have you forgotten everything completely?

ANTON: Of course not. Those were good times.

NATALIA: They were, weren't they. (*Short silence.*) I know I made you happy. That's what consoles me. Sometimes you even said (*Little laugh.*) that I inspired you.

ANTON: (*Tiredly.*) You did, dear Natalia. You did. I owe you a great deal.

Short silence.

NATALIA: I know you were young... And writers need to experience and explore...many things. I've always understood that. And then...I was really much too old for you.

ANTON: It wasn't like that.

NATALIA: I know. You don't have to tell me anything. I've always understood you better than anyone else. (*Short*

silence.) I feel...that we were perfect together. So...
perfect. (*Short silence.*) Maybe that's why you haven't
found any other woman to...share your life. (*Little
laugh.*)

ANTON: Maybe. Quite possibly. Yes...yes. It must be that.

NATALIA: If only you can tell me what I meant to you then.
I'll never ask you again.

ANTON: You were...impossible. We argued day and night.
(*Laugh.*) I needed that.

Short silence.

NATALIA: And...now?

ANTON: You're my brother's wife.

NATALIA: Is that all?

ANTON: And I'm your nice, kind brother-in-law.

Short silence.

NATALIA: Well...I really should get some sleep. (*Moves to the
door. Stops.*) You told me once that you longed to have
a child one day, so that you could teach him to love
life with all his heart and soul. But I suppose you don't
remember.

ANTON: Yes. I want my child to have a different life.

NATALIA: I've also longed for a child of my own. (*Turns.*)
Perhaps... I can find some happiness after all. The fact
is...but please don't tell Aleksander... But I think... I'm
almost sure...

ANTON: But that's wonderful.

NATALIA: I'm only sorry that you... No, never mind. (*Turns
to go.*)

ANTON: What were you going to say?

NATALIA: It's nothing. Really, it's not important.

ANTON: Tell me. I want to know.

NATALIA: (*Tearful.*) I'm sorry I ever mentioned it. It just…slipped out. (*Short silence.*) It's just that…all those precautions you told me to take…well, I never did. Forgive me, but you see…I wanted your child so desperately. For two years I hoped…but nothing happened. I thought there was something wrong with *me.*

ANTON: What are you trying to say? What are you implying?

NATALIA: I'm not implying anything.

ANTON: For once in your life, just say what you mean!

NATALIA: You don't have to shout at me. (*Short silence.*) Really…I shouldn't have to tell you. I mean…with all your…relationships…have you never had any 'trouble' of that kind?

Pause.

Well? Have you?

ANTON: No.

NATALIA: Well…surely, you must have *wondered.* I don't want to upset you. That's the last thing I want to do. After all…having a child isn't everything. There is your work. I know how much it means to you. (*Moves to the door. Turns at the door.*) And don't worry about Aleksander. I'm sure he's passed out in a ditch. (*Exits to the hall.*)

ANTON: (*Calling after her.*) Just a moment!

NATALIA: (*Appears in the doorway.*) Yes?

ANTON: There's something I want you to know. (*Getting up.*)
My brother has had a lot of misery in his life. In many
ways he's a very unfortunate man. If you can't care
about him. If you're incapable of giving him...a damn
thing! Then leave him and stop torturing him!

NATALIA: Oh, now it's me torturing him. (*Little laugh.*)

ANTON: I suppose he's angry, and I can understand why.

NATALIA: You're over-tired. I don't think you should say
any more. (*Turns to go.*)

ANTON: Don't torment my brother because you want to
punish me! Or...taunt me! I remember that disgusting
little letter you wrote me. 'Dearest Antoshevu, I'm living
with your brother. I might even sleep with him. Tell me
what you think.' It's despicable to behave like that!

NATALIA: This isn't the Anton I know. The Anton I know
would never say such things to me. (*Weeps.*)

ANTON: For God's sake, don't start. I know all your tricks!

NATALIA: How can you speak to me like that? When I was
always so kind to you. So...understanding when I never
ever...blamed you. I'm not saying another word. I only
want you to know that not many women would have
been so...sympathetic!

ANTON: Sympathetic. I see... How often could I get it up?
What was it? Only once in ten? Once in fifteen? I'm
sure you kept a count! Wrote it all down in a little black
book!

NATALIA: I never mentioned it, did I? I never said a word.

ANTON: Did you ever imagine...even for a moment...that
it could have been because of you! Who could possibly
want you? Being pawed by those bony little claws.

NATALIA: That's not true! You know it's not true!

NATALIA gives a sob, runs out and slams the door behind her.

ANTON: (*Quietly.*) Bitch, bitch, bitch, bitch.

NATALIA's hasty footsteps can faintly be heard going up the stairs. ANTON remains motionless for some moments, then he turns his head and looks at the window.

(*Quietly and bitterly.*) My God…I need air!

He crosses to the window. He lifts the net curtain and tries to open the window.

Dammit!

The window opens suddenly and ANTON leans out. There is a strong breeze and the lace curtain billows out behind him. Then, very faintly in the distance, ALEKSANDER can be heard singing the same song ('Put you wives and virgins / Under key and lock' etc). ANTON draws away from the window. The lace curtain billows out and touches his face. He turns, half stumbles to the study and closes the door behind him. As the lights fade very slowly to black, the lace curtain billows and flaps in the breeze and the song continues to drift in through the open window.

ACT THREE

When the lights come up, ALEKSANDER is standing in the dining-room door. ANTON is lying on the sofa, reading. It is two hours later and getting light. A light breeze moves the lace curtain from time to time. ALEKSANDER is carrying a rifle and his clothes are streaked with mud. He cocks the rifle and ANTON looks up. They look at each other for a few moments in silence.

ALEKSANDER: I found brother Misha snoring behind the wood-pile. I've taken away his gun. How I detest that little runt. (*Throws gun down on bed.*)

ANTON: (*Distracted. Busy reading.*) Be careful with that thing. It might go off.

ALEKSANDER: I fell asleep under a hedge. (*Yawns.*) I'm damp. Covered in mud. And I dreamt about Taganrog. I'm sorry about saying all…those things. At least you keep your head above water. Not like the rest of us. I don't know what we'd do without you. And that's the truth.

ANTON: (*Indicates his dressing-gown hanging behind the door.*) Take off your damp things. Put that on or you'll catch cold.

ALEKSANDER: Thank you doctor. (*Examines the silk dressing-gown. Looks at the label.*) Imported I see. Thanks, but I'd rather not. (*Throws dressing-gown over the back of the chaise.*) I'm encrusted with dirt and old shit. I don't bath very often. When I was stumbling about…out there in the dark, I kept thinking about my pathetic…useless life. (*Yawns and stretches.*) If it wasn't for my boys, I would have blown my brains out. In fact…I almost did!

Short silence. ANTON reads.

(*Matter of fact.*) Maybe I should just go outside and finish it.

ANTON continues to read.

(*Sarcastic.*) What are you reading?

ANTON: I'm just reading over what I've written.

ALEKSANDER: (*Sarcastic.*) So, that's why you're so enthralled.

Short silence.

ANTON: (*Distracted.*) I keep reading it over and over again. When I get to the end of a sentence...I can't remember how it begins. (*Groans.*) And the simplest words...the simplest words...as if I don't know what they mean. And the more I look at them...the more...uncanny they seem. (*Quietly.*) Uncanny. And when I get to the end of a sentence (*Passes his hand over his eyes.*) I find the full stop. Black dot. And it seems...to be getting bigger and bigger.

The following conversation/argument about ALEKSANDER's thwarted ambitions as a writer has a rather perfunctory quality. It is obviously an old issue and is being brought up to pass the time.

ALEKSANDER: My heart bleeds for you. What a tragedy it is...to be a genius. (*Short silence.*) I used to be the writer, don't you remember? *The*...writer in the family. You... traipsing after me...wanting to meet...the literary world. And you all looked up to me. Even father. You idealized me. You even started writing because you wanted to be like me. And I used to be published. Almost weekly.

ANTON: That's not quite how I remember it.

ALEKSANDER: How do you remember it?

ANTON lights a cigar.

Must you smoke those cheap cigars? The kind you find in brothels.

ANTON: I had to write…sketches, jokes, vaudevilles. No… not 'write'. Shit out. Day and night. Even when I was tired. Even when I hated it. I couldn't stop. Couldn't stop. And why? To support my family. No, no, that's not the right word. The infestation of parasites! That's why I wrote! And not…because I wanted to be like you. (*Continues to read.*)

Short silence.

ALEKSANDER: And now if one of my stories is published in some second-rate magazine, I can't even sign my own name. (*Mimicking a blustering publisher.*) 'No, no, my dear fellow. You can't possibly sign your story A. Chekhov. You might be confused with your brother (what a genius he is. If he ever has a story for me I'd be so honoured to publish it…) Oh? Well any name will do, it really doesn't matter. "Maggot", "Pussball", it really doesn't matter. You're only his brother after all.'

ANTON: And who do you have to blame for that? When I beg an editor to publish your story…

ALEKSANDER: (*Quiet and bitter.*) That's just like you. You do me a favour and then you throw it in my face! To hell with you and your 'favours'.

ANTON: …I can't even tell them that you've written it. And do you know why? Because you've cursed and insulted every bloody editor in Russia! My God, the names I've come up with. The last time it was Agathopos. I said he was Siberian. (*Laughs.*) Agathopos…Agathopos. How did I come up with that?

ALEKSANDER: I'm glad my…putrid existence amuses you!

ANTON: In fact…you've done everything…everything possible…to ruin your reputation.

ALEKSANDER: Why would I do that? Why the hell would I do that?

ANTON: (*Matter-of-fact.*) So that you can wallow in self-pity and get everyone's sympathy. My God...your life is one endless fucking catastrophe.

ALEKSANDER: (*Now more passionately.*) I'm an unfortunate person. Terrible things have happened to me. Everybody knows that. And then mother always says, (*Mimics mother.*) 'Don't pay any attention to Aleksander. He's playing up again. Why can't you be more like Antosha? He doesn't live in sin. He doesn't go blind for seven weeks from the booze. He doesn't use his children's shit-nappies for dish-cloths.'

Knock at the dining-room door. NATALIA stands in the doorway. She is dressed in a faded velvet jacket and linen skirt. She is wearing a small satin hat with a rather limp feather. She is carrying a small valise.

Why are you dressed like that? Why are you wearing a hat?

NATALIA: I've laid out the children's clothes for the funeral. Their socks are in the top drawer and their shoes are behind the door.

ALEKSANDER: Why are you telling me this?

NATALIA: Their shoes look a little scuffed. I think they need some polish. Please see to it.

ALEKSANDER: What's going on? I don't understand anything.

NATALIA: Please see that their nails are clean and that they each have a handkerchief.

ALEKSANDER: Are you going somewhere?

NATALIA: I am.

ALEKSANDER: Where the hell are you going at this time of night? Are you crazy?

NATALIA: I'm going to St Petersburg.

ALEKSANDER: St Petersburg! Now I know you're crazy!

NATALIA: I'll catch the early train. If I start walking now I'll get to the station in time. Luckily Masha has good walking shoes. They don't really fit me, but I've put paper in the toes. Please tell her that I've borrowed them and that I'll send them back.

ANTON: You can't walk all that way in the dark.

NATALIA: It's getting light. Haven't you noticed?

ANTON: You know how nervous you are and how easily frightened. You'll be all alone on a deserted farm road.

NATALIA: Nothing can be worse than staying here.

ALEKSANDER: But what's happened? It's so sudden!

NATALIA: I heard your angry voices downstairs. On and on as always. And up there, your mother moaning and crying in her sleep. I suddenly thought, 'Why do I have to be in this hell? Why do I deserve it? What does this have to do with me? Nobody even knows I exist. Nobody even wants me here.'

ALEKSANDER: But that's not true. I need you.

ANTON: You really don't have to go you know Natalia. It's not necessary.

NATALIA: (*To ALEXANDER.*) He should stay out of this. I've had quite enough of him. When he arrived, and all through dinner, he never looked at me once. I remember what I used to feel like those last months. As if I stopped existing when he didn't see me. (*Little laugh.*) Oh I know, I know I shouldn't talk about it. I became such an abject creature. I sank lower than any other woman I've ever known. But I'm sure he'll never know what that feels like.

ALEKSANDER: (*Eager to agree.*) But I'm sure he observed very closely so that he could describe it all with perfect accuracy. He's a voyeur you see. (*Moves to NATALIA.*) That valise is much too heavy for you.

NATALIA: It's heavy…but I'll manage.

ALEKSANDER: I'll carry it. I'll walk to the station with you. We can talk along the way. You can tell me what you want me to do. How I can improve myself.

NATALIA: I'm going alone. I'm sick and tired of both of you.

ALEKSANDER: Don't you have any pity? What am I going to tell my poor boys?

NATALIA: Whatever you think necessary.

ALEKSANDER: How can you do this to me now? My brother died in my arms. I'm desperately unhappy! I want to kill myself! And you just turn your back on me.

NATALIA: I have to go. (*Turning to leave.*)

ALEKSANDER: For God's sake, just listen to me! (*Wheedling.*) I'll do anything, anything, anything…

NATALIA: Let me go!

ALEKSANDER: What will I do without you?

NATALIA: Oh, I don't know. I'm sure you'll find someone else to insult and abuse.

ALEKSANDER: If you'll only let me walk you to the station. It'll be much safer that way.

NATALIA: No thank you. I know it's dangerous…but there's nothing else to be done.

ALEKSANDER: Please don't go… Don't leave me like this.

ANTON: Oh, for God's sake don't be so pathetic! If she wants to go, then let her go!

NATALIA: (*To ALEKSANDER.*) You don't deserve me and that's the truth. (*To ANTON.*) And neither does he. He drove me away! And if I think how kind I was to him. And how loyal. I never said a word to anyone.

ALEKSANDER: About what? What do you mean?

NATALIA: Never mind. Just forget it. (*Exits.*)

ALEKSANDER: (*Running after her.*) Please don't go! (*Off.*) I beg you! Please don't go! I won't let you!

NATALIA: (*Voice off.*) Take your hands off me! Just leave me alone!

ANTON sits on the sofa. He looks tired and defeated.

The sound of the front door being closed. After a while ALEKSANDER appears in the hall door. He is weeping quietly.

ALEKSANDER: What am I going to do?

ANTON: Don't worry, she'll be back. That's what she's like.

ALEKSANDER goes to the window and looks out.

ALEKSANDER: She's walking down the avenue. (*Short silence.*) You might as well know the truth. I love that woman. I love her madly, insanely. I can't live without her. (*Short silence.*) She's stopped. She's doing something to her shoe. (*Pause.*) She's beautiful, even if you don't think so. You don't see it at first…but it's true… (*Short silence.*) Now she's walking down the avenue. How can I just stand here and do nothing?

ANTON: Leave her alone. She'll come to her senses. She just wants attention. Up to her tricks. She'll be back in an hour, I promise you that.

ALEKSANDER: She's vanishing behind the trees. I feel as if I'm being left behind. As if she's taking everything with her. (*Short silence.*) That little feather in her hat makes me…indescribably sad. (*Short silence.*) She's gone. (*Turns around slowly.*) God, I'm so exhausted. I'm completely light-headed. I feel as if I'm…hallucinating.

ANTON: Stop worrying! The woman's not going anywhere. I know her.

ALEKSANDER: I'm too miserable. And why did you start shouting at her? How could you do that! Making her so unhappy. (*Weeps.*)

ANTON: I couldn't help it! I'm so sick and tired of her long-suffering bloody face. It turns my stomach! Yes. She was always so kind and sympathetic. So…understanding. My God, how that revolted me. (*Almost to himself.*) I never have any problem with whores. Give me any whore and I'll fuck her right now. It's only with the kind of woman… My God, how I hate 'respectable women' with their rancid cunts.

ALEKSANDER: You shouldn't talk like that.

ANTON: Everyone always tells me to get married to a good, decent woman. But I say I'll marry if I only have to screw the bitch once a year and if she lives five hundred miles away!

Short silence.

ALEKSANDER: Why was she different?

ANTON: Who?

ALEKSANDER: Natalia. Natalia Golden Chekhova. My...
wife! What was different about her? You banged her for
– Christ, what was it? Two years?

Pause.

What was different about her? Tell me.

Short silence.

ANTON: I...don't know. I don't know what to tell you.

ALEKSANDER: She must have been...particularly amusing?
Tell me...how did she amuse you? What... precisely...
did she do for you? I don't mind. You can be crude if
you have to.

ANTON: Oh, for Christ's sake, it's all in the past. What does
it matter. Let's not talk about it. Please just let it go.

ALEKSANDER: I can't let it go! (*Quietly.*) Damn you. I can't
let it go.

Short silence.

ANTON: I suppose my miserable, senseless life has made
me...callous. Yes, it's true. For years I haven't really
cared about a woman. Because of the way I live...I've
become a coarse and vulgar man. (*Pause.*) I don't think
I could ever really care about another human being.
(*Pause.*) And maybe I don't want anyone to care about
me. God no. Above all, not that. (*Pause.*) The only thing
that still interests me...is life. Beautiful...grotesque...
absurd.

ALEKSANDER: Well...for me...life is one long fucking
misery. Christ, I've just found a woman...and now she's
gone off and left me. I've only known one misfortune
after another. I was treated like...filth since the day
I was born. Sometimes...I don't even know why I'm
still alive. Why I don't...just put an end to it all. Just
once and for all. (*Pause.*) I'm thirty-four. If I live until

I'm sixty-four... I'll have to be miserable for another thirty years. I've been miserable since I can remember. Nothing's really changed. Often I get just as frightened when I have to go to sleep. Just as frightened as I used to get...in Taganrog. (*Pause.*) I tell myself it's childish. That there's no reason. (*Pause.*) But it doesn't help. (*Pause.*) It happened again about a week ago. I buried my head under the pillow. Began crying with agony. The more I cried, the worse it got. I was overcome...by despair. I got up, got dressed and went out into the street. I was frightened of everything. Of the people passing by. Of the street-car bells. Of every noise. I went into a tavern and drank some vodka. It didn't help. Then I walked on until I got to an old bridge. I took off my jacket and my shirt I exposed my chest to the icy wind. But that didn't help either. Nothing helps! (*Short silence.*) Here I am. Thirty-four years old. I'm supposed to be a man. But I'm not. I'm still that pitiful little boy. (*Short silence.*) And to think that Kolia wanted to go back there... To where we were so miserable. (*Pause.*) The morning before he died...I sat with him and all he spoke about was Taganrog. He wanted to write everything down. Everything he remembered.

ANTON: What did he say? (*Sits on the edge of the bed.*)

ALEKSANDER: How we used to go to the old Quarantine cemetery to dig up skulls.

ANTON: (*Musing.*) That's where I caught spiders. With balls of wax. What else?

ALEKSANDER: The stories you told us when we couldn't sleep.

ANTON: After you were both asleep...I'd go on telling the story...on and on...to comfort myself. (*Short laugh.*)

Short silence.

ALEKSANDER How you shot finches. Trapped starlings.

ANTON: Oh God...those finches. I don't want to think about them. And how the wounded ones used to screech all night in their cages. (*Pause.*) And the starlings with their broken wings. I think I can still hear them. (*Pause.*) I'll never get away from that sound.

ALEKSANDER: He didn't even mention the thrashings. Odd that he spoke of so many nice things. The pretty girls. The river in the evening. The lime trees blossoming.

ANTON: (*Quietly.*) Maybe that's all one keeps in the end. At least, one hopes so. (*Short silence.*) But...I can't really believe that. *I'll* never forget. Not until my dying day. (*Short silence.*) I'll never forget when father began to 'teach' me as he called it. Beating me when I was four years old. Thrashing me with a cane. Twisting my arm. Punching my head. Every morning when I woke up...I wondered if I would be beaten today. (*Short silence.*) It still torments me. Look. (*Holds up his hand.*) Just thinking about it...makes me tremble.

ALEKSANDER: You don't have to tell me. (*Pause.*) Why don't you at least get angry? Why don't you rage and curse like I do? Always so calm. Amused. Above it all. Even when we were small. It used to make me sick and afraid to see your calm, white face. I wish you would let it out, for once. Just shit it all out. (*Short silence.*) It was hell, wasn't it!

ANTON: Sheer hell. (*Pause.*) Without a glimmer of light. (*Pause.*) I can still feel it. Almost smell it. That... crushing anguish. Let's not dwell on it. What's the use?

ALEKSANDER: Like being at the bottom of a dark...dank well.

ANTON: Yes. (*Pause.*) Like that. (*Pause.*) I still suffer from insomnia. I never wanted to go to sleep. If I slept I would have to wake up the next day. (*Pause.*) And I didn't want that. (*Pause.*) In the dark...I sometimes feel as if cobwebs are covering my face. The cobwebs we used to have in every corner of our house. (*Wiping his palm over his eyes.*) I still...dream about Taganrog.

ALEKSANDER: Do you?

ANTON: It never goes away. Never. Never. (*Faltering.*) I dream...about the house...in Moiseev Street. Particularly...one dream. Over and over again. That corridor leading to the little room where we slept. Long...dark... narrow. Death-watch beetles...ticking... ticking like clocks.

ALEKSANDER: Tell me about the dream.

ANTON: I don't want to think about it.

ALEKSANDER: Please.

ANTON: No! (*Quietly.*) No. (*Short silence.*) It...didn't look bad from the street. Painted walls. Lace curtains. Mother looking out. Watching the tumbrils with the criminals coming into the square. Their hands tied behind their backs. Drums rolling. Terrible drums. While she sucked those endless boiled sweets. A real parlour...with upholstered chairs...ghastly wallpaper...gaslight...and even a piano.

ALEKSANDER: Don't tell me – I don't want to remember. (*Closing his eyes, as if in pain.*) We were never allowed in there. And no one played the piano.

ANTON: But...behind that...behind that. (*Growing distressed.*) At the back... Cockroach infested rooms. Broken windows...rising damp... Stinking sewers... Bedbugs...breeding in the cracks. Doors... Shutters... Hanging off their hinges. Banging...banging...all night. And that dark upstairs room...where our little sister died...slowly...slowly. 'Come and say goodbye. Come and say goodbye to your sister.' Small, pale face in a lace bonnet. Mother gasping and weeping… Kissing that cold, cold skin.

ALEKSANDER: You mustn't think about it!

ANTON: The lamp smoking… A staring doll at the bottom of the bed. And the store…the store where father used to thrash us. Old linoleum… Rancid dripping… Sound of him…bending and unbending the cane. Clearing his throat. Once I saw our mother… watching through a crack in the door. Her face…quite still.

ALEKSANDER: My God. Don't tell me – why did you have to tell me that?

ANTON: And down in the shop… From dawn to midnight. (*Mimicking father.*) 'I never had a childhood. Why should you?' Picking grubs out of the flour. Fishing dead rats out of the oil. Selling 'bird's nest' mixture to all those scared, pathetic women. So desperate to abort those foetuses… (*His voice trembles.*) But…in one of the… dingiest rooms…three small brothers…share a sagging double bed. The feather mattress smells of stale piss.

ALEKSANDER: Be quiet for God's sake! I don't want to hear any more. (*Moves to the door.*)

ANTON: You stay where you are! And you listen to me! You wanted to know!

ALEKSANDER is taken aback and sits down.

Only one…flickering candle. Giving off…a sulphurous light. A sickening…sickening light. Always…hungry… unhappy. Afraid to sleep…and dream. Afraid…to wake up. Above all…always…always…unbearably alone. (*Breaks down and weeps. Stops almost at once. Softly, quickly. Almost feverishly.*) Do you remember the rats in that house? Everywhere. Snap of rat-trap? Cracking rat spines. Rat droppings. Rat piss. Cats eating rats. Rat guts. Rat heads. Rat's teeth in the stew. Rats up in the ceiling. Under the beds. Bed-legs in paraffin so that rats won't climb up. Gnaw their way into our anuses. In gutters…drains. Burning…tiny…frightened eyes. So many…so many of them. Rats…rats…rats…

ALEKSANDER: (*Crosses to ANTON.*) It's alright, it's alright. (*Sits next to him and puts his arm around his shoulders.*) Leave it now. Leave it. (*Long silence. Both staring at the floor.*)

ANTON: (*Whispers brokenly.*) Taganrog.

ALEKSANDER: (*Whispers.*) Yes. I know. I know. (*Pause.*) I hated you sometimes…for being so… You know… For refusing to show…

ANTON: I know.

ALEKSANDER: (*Removing his arm. Suddenly hearty.*) Now we can really talk to each other. Share things!

ANTON: (*Sad smile. Then quietly.*) I've always cared about you, Aleksander. Maybe more than about anyone else.

ALEKSANDER: I suppose I've always known that. You've always been so good to me.

ALEKSANDER turns his head and looks at the window. ANTON watches him.

ANTON: (*Quietly.*) I suppose you want to go and look for her?

ALEKSANDER: (*Slightly sheepish.*) Well…maybe I should. It's…very dark out there. (*Short silence.*) Thank you, Antosha. I can't tell you what it means to me.

ANTON: And I've always relied on your honesty. More than I can say.

ALEKSANDER: Well! Things will be different from now on! This is…a new beginning!

ANTON: (*Slowly rises and crosses to the window. Short silence. Looks out.*) I don't think I'll be seeing you again.

ALEKSANDER: But why not? Are you going away? For God's sake what do you mean? Where are you going?

ANTON: Or, at least…never quite as closely and as clearly as I'm seeing you now. (*Turns to face him.*)

ALEKSANDER: What are you saying?

ANTON: Already… I imagine…you're moving a little away from me. Quite slowly. Like being on a boat.

ALEKSANDER: You're frightening me. I'm here! As large as life.

ANTON: And you will probably continue to move away. Further and further. (*Wipes his hand over his eyes.*) Until I can't see you at all.

ALEKSANDER: What's happened to you?

ANTON: (*Passionately.*) Do you think it's what I want? To be even more…Godforsaken and alone!!

ALEKSANDER: Then why are you saying these terrible things? Stop it!

ANTON: (*Despairingly.*) There's nothing I can do. I believe that you won't be able to help it. You've always been *at* me, haven't you? *At* me. Wanting to see…if I also…have that place inside me. And now you know! (*Knocks against his chest.*) Yes! It's here! All of it! Every stinking piece… collected and…intact. And now every time you see me…I'll remind you of it. And so…you'll have to leave me behind. Because you can't bear it. And of course I understand. No one (*Laughs.*) understands better than I do.

ALEKSANDER: It's not true.

ANTON: Isn't it?

ALEKSANDER: I'll forget. I promise. I've forgotten already.

ANTON: (*Quietly and sadly.*) And are you satisfied now?
Since I can remember you've been prodding, preying.
Trying to find out. The *true* Anton Pavlovich. And...
there...we are.

ALEKSANDER: I only wanted to get close to you. Please
understand that. Please understand. To share things with
you.

Silence. ANTON shuts his eyes.

ANTON: (*Quietly, painfully. Speaking with closed eyes.*) But
it would happen gradually. We'd hardly notice or
remember why. And it wouldn't even hurt. That is the
worst of it.

ALEKSANDER: I've told you it's not true!

ANTON: *I* know it is. And *you* know it is. Surely you know
yourself. How you're always running away. Always.
Running away...from this. (*Short silence.*) And there's
nothing we can do about it.

ALEKSANDER: (*Brokenly.*) Don't say these things.

ANTON: (*Quietly.*) I'm sorry.

ALEKSANDER: (*Starts weeping.*) Oh, God. Holy Mother of
God.

ANTON crosses to ALEKSANDER and crouches next to him.

ANTON: (*With extreme sadness.*) You think that at last this
is my truth? (*Touches his chest.*) This...abyss of horrors?
It's just the opposite. I'll tell you what it really is. I'll
tell you. My *truth*...is the deliberate...intricate...and
perfectly elegant...plot...that I construct...in *place* of
this. That is my truth.

*The front door bangs. Sound of NATALIA approaching. ANTON
slowly rises to his feet. A knock at the open hall door. NATALIA
stands in the doorway. She looks tired and dishevelled. She
is still wearing a hat and carrying her valise.*

NATALIA: I'm not staying. Don't think I'm staying. It's just
that…I'm so terribly tired. I think it's…much too far for
me to walk.

Silence.

In a little while I'll start asking around to see if anyone
can take me into town.

*Short silence. NATALIA keeps standing in the doorway. She
looks acutely uncomfortable.*

What's the matter with the two of you?

ANTON: (*Kindly.*) Come in and sit down.

*NATALIA sits down gingerly on the edge. She puts her valise
down next to her. ALEKSANDER gets up. Crosses to her, sits,
takes her hand.*

NATALIA: (*Pulling her hand away.*) My feet hurt so terribly.
The shoes…are much too big for me. (*Takes her shoes off.*)
Just look at my heel. It's bleeding.

ALEKSANDER: (*Sincerely.*) You should ask my brother. He's a
doctor. He'll know what to do.

ANTON crosses to her.

ANTON: Let me see. (*Crouches next to her. Takes her foot in his
hand and examines her heel.*) I'll have to put something on
that. (*Gets up and rummages in his doctor's bag.*)

Awkward silence.

NATALIA: (*To ALEKSANDER.*) And where have you been
sleeping? Just look at you.

ALEKSANDER: Under a hedge.

NATALIA: You're covered in mud. It must have been damp. I hope you haven't made yourself ill.

ALEKSANDER: Don't worry. You know how tough I am.

ANTON crosses to her and crouches next to her. He has a bottle of iodine and some cotton-wool. NATALIA lifts her foot.

ANTON: It burns. But not for long. (*He dabs iodine on her heel.*)

NATALIA: (*Gasps.*) Oh, blow on it please! It hurts!

ANTON: (*Blows on her heel.*) In a little while, I'll put on a plaster. (*Gets up and puts the iodine back in the doctor's bag.*)

ALEKSANDER: You should never have gone! You don't know how many ruffians and scoundrels are out there!

Awkward silence.

NATALIA: (*Pointedly to ALEKSANDER.*) When I got to that avenue of trees… (*Points to the window.*) my feet started hurting and I said to myself, 'I'll count to five and if a bird sings then I'll turn back.' When I got to 'four' a large bird flew up right in front of me. (*Short silence.*) Right in front of me.

ANTON goes to the window and looks out. ALEKSANDER watches him furtively, almost shyly, as if he's seeing him for the first time.

ANTON: (*After a silence.*) It's getting light.

ALEKSANDER: It must be almost morning. (*Wipes his nose on the back of his sleeve.*)

Short silence.

What's the time?

ANTON: I don't know. At one of those Godforsaken stations I lost my pocket-watch.

ALEKSANDER: Odd, I've also been losing things. In three days I've lost a button, a comb and a fountain-pen. (*Short silence.*) Imagine that.

Silence.

When is the funeral?

ANTON: At seven.

ALEKSANDER: So early.

ANTON: They said it had to be. It's because of the heat.

ALEKSANDER: Oh. (*Pause.*) I see.

Short silence.

ANTON: How I dread it. Soon…it's all going to start.

ALEKSANDER: Yes.

A loud knocking at the front door.

ANTON: I'll go. (*He exits to the hall.*)

Silence as ALEKSANDER and NATALIA listen. The sound of the front door being opened and then a gruff voice talking outside. Throughout the next scene, an inaudible conversation between ANTON and the gruff-voiced man can faintly be heard in the background.

ALEKSANDER: Tell me one thing. I have to know.

NATALIA: What?

Pause.

ALEKSANDER: Do you still want him? After everything?

Pause.

NATALIA: No. It's finished for me.

ALEKSANDER: Are you sure?

NATALIA: Quite sure.

ALEKSANDER: Well, thank God for that. Maybe…at last…
you'll be able to care about me.

Pause.

NATALIA: No. I don't think so.

ALEKSANDER: What do you mean?

NATALIA: I thought I could…learn to care for you. (*Pause.*) I
was wrong.

ALEKSANDER: But I love you!

NATALIA: I don't think you do. I think…you only wanted
me to prefer you to him.

ALEKSANDER: That's not true!

Short silence.

NATALIA: I used to care for him, but now…I don't have any
feelings for either of you.

ALEKSANDER: (*Brokenly.*) My God. (*Short silence.*) What are
we going to do?

NATALIA: I don't know. (*Short silence.*) If I left you…

ALEKSANDER: Don't leave me. Please.

NATALIA: I'm not young any more. I've lost my looks.

Sound of the front door closing.

And I don't have any money.

The sound of ANTON's footsteps approaching.

ANTON: (*Entering.*) It was the man with the wagon. A real
oaf. He wants to nail up the coffin…so that they can
load it. (*Pause.*) I told them (*Gestures towards the bedroom*

door.) they should go round to the outside door. (*Pause.*)
He proudly showed me the hideous wreath they're
going to put on the coffin. A bloody great gilt and black
thing. (*Pause.*) He says the Lintvariovs are coming in
their carriage. Masha and mother will ride with them.

ALEKSANDER: And what about us?

ANTON: I suppose we'll have to walk.

ALEKSANDER: But the church is almost a mile away.

NATALIA: (*Long-suffering.*) Now that I'm still here, I suppose
I'll have to go. But how will I get there? My feet are
hurting. Your mother and sister dislike me. They won't
let me ride with them. You know how…spiteful they can
be.

ALEKSANDER: Oh, let's not talk about it now!

*Sound of male voices in the bedroom. They look towards the
bedroom.*

ANTON: How Kolia would have hated all this…pomposity.
He would have preferred some wild…and drunken
party. With enough booze and opium for all his
disgusting friends. (*Laugh.*)

ALEKSANDER: God…what a bunch. (*Laugh.*)

ANTON: Screaming and fighting, singing and puking. And
when they're completely pissed…one of them always
plays a balalaika and they start dancing! (*Laugh.*)

ALEKSANDER: Like lunatics! (*Illustrates.*)

ANTON: Staggering…and thrashing! Crashing into each
other! Breaking the windows and the furniture!

*ALEKSANDER tries to sing one of their songs. Can't remember
it. ANTON and ALEKSANDER laugh and then fall silent.*

ALEKSANDER: (*Picking up the violin.*) I promised mother I'd put this in the coffin with him. But I'm not going to. Kolia wouldn't want that.

Voices off. The odd thud and moving of furniture. ALEKSANDER draws the bow softly over the strings. It makes an eerie sound.

He played so beautifully. And when he played…his whole face just lit up.

ALEKSANDER continues to draw the bow over the strings.

He could write…he was a musician…a painter. And what did he do?…pissed it against the wall. Kolia my brother. My poor brother. What a life. He was always searching for his identity papers and sometimes couldn't even remember where he'd slept for the last three weeks.

ALEKSANDER puts the violin and the bow down.

NATALIA: (*Sad.*) But for all that…he was a kind man. A sweet…kind man.

Sound of hammering of coffin lid.

ALEKSANDER: They're closing him up.

Remorseless sound of the repetitive hammering continues until otherwise indicated in the text.

ALEKSANDER: (*Suddenly shouts to bedroom.*) Leave him alone damn you! It's not time yet!

ANTON: (*Resigned.*) Let them get on with it. It's got to be done.

ALEKSANDER stares sadly at the bedroom door.

ALEKSANDER: They're closing him up. I'll never see him again. Never again.

ALEKSANDER crosses to the bed and sits down. They are all completely still as they listen to the hammering. The hammering stops and the voices recede.

ANTON: I'm going for a walk. (*Gets up and exits rapidly.*)

ALEKSANDER: Never see…that funny face of his. (*Weeps. Covers his face with his hands.*)

Silence.

(*Still with his face in his hands.*) Can't you see how I'm suffering? How miserable I am? Won't you take pity on me?

Silence.

(*Lifts his face.*) Natalia…for God's sake…just look at me.

NATALIA averts her face.

There's…nothing left of me.

Short silence. NATALIA is still averting her face.

I know you don't love me. And you'll probably never love me… (*Pause.*) I know you think I don't deserve you. And I don't blame you. I mean…just look at me. I'm a misery. (*Pause.*) All I want is to have you near me. That's all. I won't ask you…to care about me. I won't ask anything. (*Pause.*) Just…stay with me. Please. I can't bear to live alone. I can't bear it. Please. Please say you will. Please, please say it. I beg you.

In the silence some distance away, the sound of many male voices raised up in song. This sonorous singing continues until the end of the play.

NATALIA: Yes. I'll stay.

ALEKSANDER: Thank God for that.

NATALIA bursts into tears and hides her face in her hands.

Sound of hasty footsteps. ANTON appears in the door.

ANTON: You won't believe what I've just seen! You won't believe it!

ALEKSANDER: (*Looking up slowly.*) What?

ANTON: People! Hundreds of people! In the paddock! My God, there must be three hundred at least. And there are still more...they're coming from everywhere! (*Laughs.*)

ALEKSANDER: But what are they doing here?

ANTON: All clutching their cheap icons! Grandfathers on home-made crutches, women suckling their young, men wearing felt boots... All waiting...to walk in a procession to the church! Behind Kolia's coffin! (*Laughs.*)

ALEKSANDER: I can't believe it!

ANTON: My God... It's not just a procession... It's a bloody pageant! Kolia! (*Rushes to the bedroom door.*) Do you hear, brother? A fucking Tzar! You're going to have a funeral...fit for a fucking Tzar! A fucking Tzar! (*Laughs. To ALEKSANDER.*) You must come and see.

ALEKSANDER: But how did it happen? They don't even know him.

ANTON: They told me it's because our rich friends the Lintvariovs let it be known that every peasant who walks in the procession will be rewarded with (*Formal voice.*) – 'a head-scarf, a glass of vodka – and...a pork-pie!'

They both laugh uproariously. The sound of sonorous male voices raised in song.

Listen to them. They're singing a hymn for us. So that...they told me...we will be blessed and comforted.

ALEKSANDER: We used to have processions like this in
Taganrog. Don't you remember? Peasants with icons
following the coffin. It was the custom there!

ANTON: Of course. The procession used to go from
the church to the old cemetery. (*Laugh.*) Amazing!
(*Pause.*) Come and see! Natalia! It's all so wonderfully
ridiculous!

*NATALIA hesitates. She looks at ANTON for a moment. Then
she gets up and exits rapidly.*

Put your shoes on. They expect us to be respectable!
(*Laughs.*) After all, it's a great occasion! Around here,
everyone will talk about it for years and years! The
magnificent funeral of Kolia Chekhov! (*Exits.*)

*ALEKSANDER starts looking for his shoes. He finds one and
puts it on.*

ALEKSANDER: (*Looks for his other shoe.*) Oh, to hell with it!

Wearing only one shoe, he hobbles to the hall door.

Wait for me! (*Almost desperately.*) Wait for me!

*As the lights fade quickly to black, the singing is brought up
loudly and heard for moments in the black.*